Dedication

Special thanks to my best friend and my AMAZING wife, Autumn Berrier.

Photographer: Autumn Harrison Photography

Special thanks my beautiful daughter Lana Harrison.

Special thanks to Callye Keen for being one of the best friends a guy could ask for. Callye is the reason this book was ever born.

Special thanks to my father and mother, Don Berrier and Harriett Childress.

Special thanks to my brother Josh Berrier

Special thanks to my brother from another mother, Nick Jones.

Special thanks to Mike Cludio, Brad Lea, Roger Wakefield, Caleb Feyereisen and Ryan Wheeler for being friends and mentors of mine and have provided immense value to my life.

Thank you to everyone else that was a part in this book.

9 SIMPLE STEPS TO

SELL MORE $H!T

Shatter stereotypes, annihilate sales records and transform your business from surviving to **THRIVING!**

COREY BERRIER

9 Simple Step to Sell More $h!ts

Quantity sales and special discounts are available on quantity purchases by corporations, associations, and others. For details, contact the publisher at the address above.

Orders by U.S. trade bookstores and wholesalers. Email info@BeyondPublishing.net

The Beyond Publishing Speakers Bureau can bring authors to your live event. For more information or to book an event contact the Beyond Publishing Speakers Bureau speak@BeyondPublishing.net

The Author can be reached directly at BeyondPublishing.net

Manufactured and printed in the United States of America distributed globally by BeyondPublishing.net

New York | Los Angeles | London | Sydney

ISBN Softcover: 978-1-63792-400-6

ISBN Hardcover: 978-1-63792-428-0

contents

WRITTEN BY: **COREY BERRIER** - DESIGN BY: **SOUL OR FLARE**

introduction

If you don't know who I am, my name is **Corey Berrier**. I am a (SME) Subject Matter Expert with over 25 years of experience training
individuals and teams on high performance sales processes. I've developed a proprietary system to guide businesses and entrepreneurs to higher sales results, focusing on every aspect from start to finish.

I always use a hands-on approach, with feedback provided throughout the entire process, helping clients achieve their desired results faster. Our proven results have helped hundreds of professionals across multiple industries achieve improved sales results.

With any career there is usually a stereotype (or two) associated with it, and salespeople definitely got the short end of that stick. Some struggle to combat this preconceived notion, while others simply overlook the holes in their systems. My job is to figure out those holes, identify the real problem rather than the symptoms. In this guide I give you nine actionable steps to help you reach your maximum potential. So, **let's get started**!

#1 confidence to close

When I was in sixth grade, I was invited to a pool party. Sounds like a great time, right? I thought so - especially when the three cutest girls in the WHOLE school started walking towards me. I knew I had a few extra pounds on me, but I shook off my self-doubt, took a few deep breaths and tried to work up the confidence to talk to them.

Turns out they actually had something to ask me; they asked me if **I needed a training bra**. In front of the whole class.

My confidence was instantly destroyed.

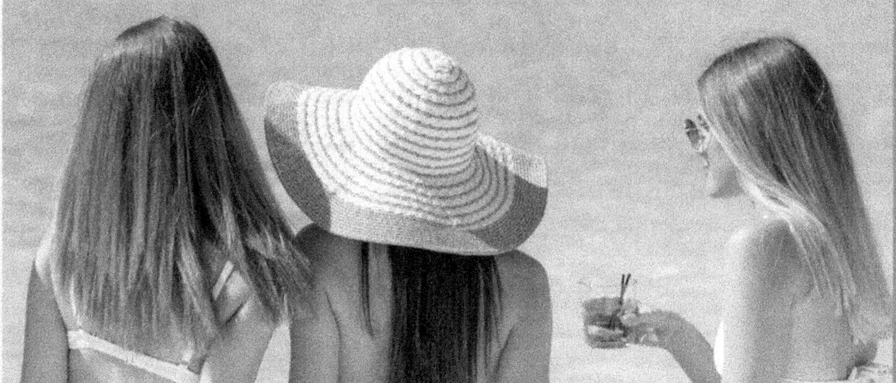

The first one is simple; **it could have ruined my life**. Dramatic? Yes. But come on.... I was in sixth grade! When I think back on that night now, it seems trivial... and they absolutely could have said something much worse. But with hormones raging and social pressure amping up more with each generation, sometimes a simple sentence can throw a person right off their path. It could have spiraled me into a deep depression. I could have continued to use food as a crutch and a coping mechanism. I could've avoided as many social interactions as possible to make sure I never encountered a situation like that again. It can be extremely difficult to recover when your confidence takes a blow (and even harder if you're a teenager).

Luckily for me, I chose the second option. That night marked a starting point for me to take back control of my mind and body.

I used that night as **fuel** to never be fat again.

This story is a great example of how important but fragile confidence is. And of course, confidence is an essential trait to have if you are in sales.

One of the most important things a salesperson can do is believe in themselves and their product or service. If you don't believe in what you're selling, no one else will. If you are in a room with ten other people selling the same thing as you, what makes those potential clients choose to approach you? Why should someone listen to you? If you can't answer that question immediately after hearing it, we have some work to do! And, we'll start with the **three most common obstacles** when it comes to building **unbreakable confidence**:

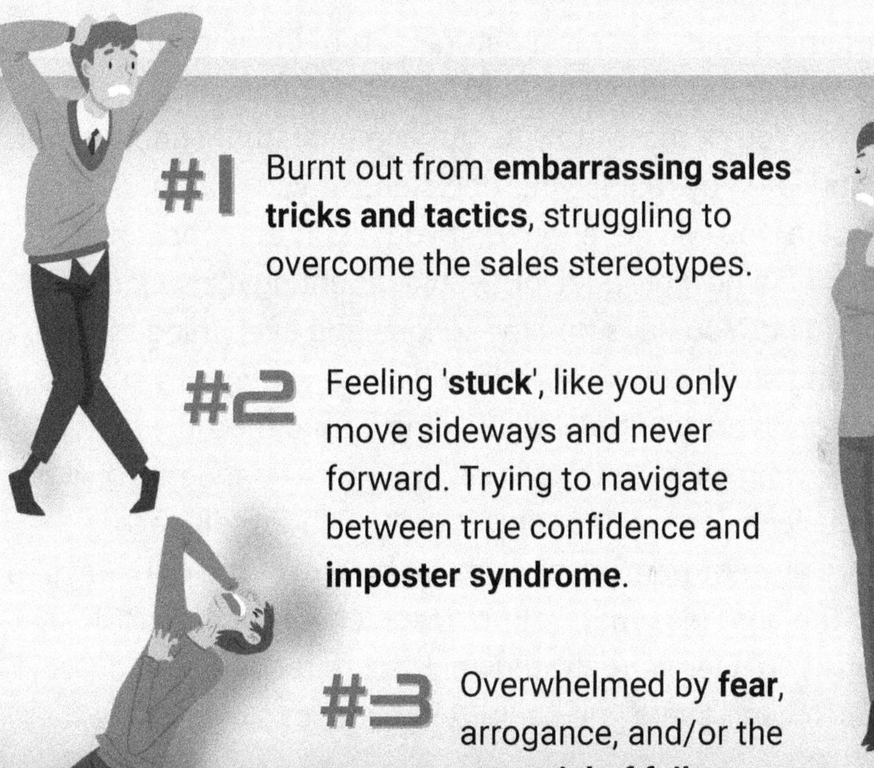

#1 Burnt out from **embarrassing sales tricks and tactics**, struggling to overcome the sales stereotypes.

#2 Feeling '**stuck**', like you only move sideways and never forward. Trying to navigate between true confidence and **imposter syndrome**.

#3 Overwhelmed by **fear**, arrogance, and/or the **potential of failure**.

Do you relate to any of those struggles I just mentioned? Confidence is a pretty broad term and it means something different to each person. It also presents very differently from one person to another. But how can be sure that **you** are confident? Maybe you feel like you are not and never will be a confident person? If that sounds like you, I need to tell you something; you need to let that thought go out of your mind and never let it back in.

Confidence is not a mysterious quality that only some lucky people are born with. It's a learned behavior - and it's yours for the taking. You **can** build unbreakable confidence, and use it to maximize your business' potential. So how can you do it?

Overcome Fear! - Fear is a natural part of life and business. It's also a common obstacle to building confidence. It can paralyze you or motivate you, but one thing that should never be motivated by fear is your decisions. If you fear the unknown, you will never grow. If you are in the process of launching a new product, but you're doubting it's success, keep going! You have nothing to lose and everything to gain by taking small steps towards achieving your goal's success. The more work you put into building confidence in yourself and growing as an entrepreneur, the more confident you'll be, and the less you will fear opportunity. Fear of failure is extremely common, but failure can be one of the only ways to learn the hard lessons. Failure doesn't mean you can't do it; it means you need to restrategize. Start to recognize your fears and see what steps you can put into place to over come them.

Now, onto the opposite of fear - **love**! Think of all the things you love about yourself. Write them down, and keep that list somewhere close by for easy reference. When you're feeling down and low about your confidence, take a look at this list and remind yourself of how great you are! You can also use this as a tool when people try to tear down your self-esteem: just remember all the wonderful qualities in yourself that aren't necessarily visible to others. For some this exercise will be extremely easy. For others, it may be one of the hardest things to do. We are trained not to brag about how great we are, but that is exactly what I want you to do. I'm not asking you to write a romance novel to yourself; it can be as simple as a list of words that you associate with who you truly are.

While we're writing things down, it can be a great exercise to keep a **journal of your wins** - big and small. It's important to have a record of what you have achieved to then reference and use as motivation for the future. In addition to writing down your past wins, write down your goals for the future and how you are going to achieve them. What qualities do you have that will make it easier/harder to achieve? What systems can you put into place to help you achieve your goals in the most effective way? You are an expert at yourself (whether you think so or not). Start to get introspective! Once you start tracking your wins and goals, set reminders for yourself so that when you look back at your journal in a few months, it will remind you of all the progress made.

Surround yourself with the right people and things. This is a tough one, because sometimes the things and people we love most are not always the best to be around when starting or growing a business. Be careful who you choose as friends, especially when it comes to people who are negative or critical of your goals and ambitions. The same goes for what type of media you consume (especially social media). Try to remember that everything your seeing on ANYONE'S social media accounts is simply a highlight reel; **we only see what people want us to see**. Never compare yourself to another person's highlight reel - especially in business. I have found that the people who are truly successful are those who speak the least about it online.

I'm going to keep this part somewhat general and vague, probably because I could write a whole separate book about it. **Make healthy choices**. When you make healthy choices you feel better. When you feel better, you **work better**. All of these things add together to help build your unbreakable confidence. If you have a bad habit, do whatever you can to overcome it. If you want to succeed in your business a bad habit is certainly not going to make it easier.
Trust me.

Plus, imagine the confidence you
can gain by overcoming a habit
that is only slowing you down!

Confidence has become something of a buzz word these days. When it comes to sales, this confidence can be easily mistaken for arrogance, since there are so many preconceived notions about the dreaded 'salesperson'. A concept that can be quite helpful is this: the word '**trust**' can be used interchangeably with the word 'confidence'. When you trust yourself, you are confident in your abilities. They go hand in hand. So, how do you use your **unbreakable confidence** to close deals?

- Be **yourself** — You've heard this probably too many times to count, but in business this is extremely important. Don't try to be something or someone else. Be yourself so people can get to know and like you for who you actually are. Plus, it's a lot easier to be yourself than anyone else.

- Be **clear** — Listen carefully when prospects and customers are talking, so that nothing gets lost in translation. This will help avoid misunderstandings down the line when negotiating deals or delivering the services or products promised during initial sales pitch meeting(s).

- Be **prepared** — Research ahead of time to prepare for any meeting or event. Have all necessary documents ready before any meetings so there aren't any delays caused last minute scrambling. Prepare ahead of time to best avoid anything that would throw off your confidence.

unbreakable confidence

WHAT DO YOU WANT?

WHO ARE YOU WHEN NO ONE IS AROUND?

DO YOU BELIEVE WHAT YOU DO MATTERS?

WHAT DOES SUCCESS LOOK LIKE FOR YOU?

PRACTICE = CONFIDENCE

know your customer

Why is knowing your customer so important in sales? I can tell you in one sentence: **we spent $10,000 on ads targeting the wrong people**. Can you imagine how frustrating that was?

If you don't know **who** your ideal customer is, you're going to waste a LOT of time, effort and money trying to convince those people to buy what you're selling. If you have a solid understanding of who your perfect audience is, where they are most likely to spend their time (and see your content), you may have people asking **YOU** how they can buy what you're selling. Which would you prefer?

Knowing your customer is vital to building a successful sales strategy. It's easy to assume that everyone wants the same thing, but in reality, each person has their own specific needs and desires for their product. For example, some people may be looking for something that will help them save time or money; others may want something that makes them feel good about themselves or helps them get ahead at work. Still, others might just need it because they've always wanted one!

No matter what product or service you're selling, you need to understand what your target market wants out of it. If you don't know who they are and what they're looking for, then how can you expect to sell them anything?

Not having a solid understanding on a target customer is one of, if not the most common struggle with businesses. I see it all the time, and it is always the first place to look; if you're selling to the wrong people, it doesn't matter how great your product or your service is. There are a few reasons that this happens, but it really all comes down to where you're focused.

self-focused

Selling what you want (or think people want) not what your customers actually NEED. Just because you think it's a great idea doesn't mean it is...(unfortunately).

unaware

Offering everything without any knowledge of what works. Putting too much energy and money in the wrong places You may feel like you never know where to focus.

tunnel vision

Failing to assess the industry, competition and anything outside of your business. Without this knowledge, you wont know how best to communicate to your customers that **you** are the best option for them.

There are about a million different ways to really understand who your target customer is.. and too many options almost always causes decision paralysis. I like to keep it simple to 5 easy categories:

WHO is your ideal customer?

WHAT problem(s) does your product/service solve for them?

WHERE can you find these ideal customers?

HOW will you attract them? How will you connect with them?

WHY will they want to become a customer? Why will they choose you over your competition?

Answer these questions in detail and you will save yourself an enormous amount of time and money. The exponential success your business will see is just the icing on the cake.

Remember: the more you know, the better you can target and communicate exactly how you intend to - to the people who are most likely to do business with you.

know your customer

WHO IS YOUR PERFECT CUSTOMER?

WHAT ARE THEIR PAIN POINTS?

WHY ARE YOU THE BEST PERSON TO HELP THEM?

WHO IS YOUR COMPETITION?

WHAT DO THEY DO THAT WORKS? WHAT DOESN'T WORK?

ARE THEY WINNING? WHY?

I have a cold hard fact for you; you don't have to love prospecting (most don't), but **you still have to do it**. And here's one fun fact: if you completed step two effectively, this process becomes a LOT easier.

The prospecting process is a critical part of building your business, but it's often under-appreciated and under-utilized. As technology and business continue to merge and advance, prospects don't just want to buy from you, they want to become part of your story. Your story is your unique **value proposition** — it's what sets you apart from the competition and makes people want to do business with you. But, before you can tell anyone else your story, you have to know what it is and why it matters. Once you know it, that's where marketing comes in: it's the **art of connecting people with their values** by telling stories that resonate with them. It's how you craft your message to best communicate with the people who need it.

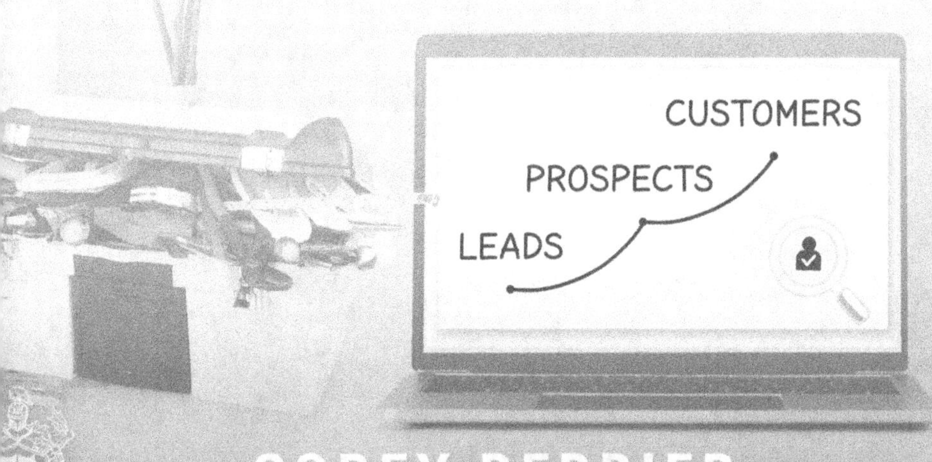

Being **Unheard**
Casting a big net without catching a thing. Your message isn't resonating.

Spammer
You outreach is annoying not attracting customers. Instead of listening, they are waiting for you to stop talking.

Fear of **No**
Fear of objections can lead to steamrolling through the process - which never builds a brand and rarely gets sales.

The choice is yours; do you want to stay guessing when the next call is coming? Or master a process of getting customers yourself? And for those of you out there who need to hear it...

NOT EVERYONE IS A QUALIFIED PROSPECT.

Chase the wrong people and get the opposite results you're looking for. It really is that simple.

COREY BERRIER

Imagine cutting through the sea of noise to speak with an audience hungry for your business. Imagine collaborating with customers to grow a business into a brand and into a movement. Imagine resonating so well with your customers that they become a separate (and free) marketing machine.

Too good to be true? Absolutely not.

Here are the best strategies to gain absolute focus with your target audience:

Friction and Fears

One of the #1 reasons prospects don't buy is **fear**. They may have had a bad past experience, or they may just be naturally skeptical about making any kind of commitment. Either way, you need to **address these fears** in the first point of contact you make with your potential customers.

Experts and Gurus

If a prospect feels like they (or a competitor) know more than you do about the product and service you're offering, you need to prove them wrong. Show them that your expertise will help them achieve their goals more easily than if they did it themselves or with someone else.

Tools of the Trade

You can't sell without knowing what works best for your prospect's industry, finances and personal preferences — but how do you find out all this information in order to build a relationship with them? Tools like LinkedIn, Google alerts and Twitter are great at keeping tabs on what's happening in your industry — but they're even better at helping you find out what really matters most in your target market.

Questions and Searches

Ask questions and search online for answers. This is the quickest way to gain knowledge about your industry. It will also help you create better products that people want and need. This tip leads perfectly into my next one…

Groups and Forums

Meet your customers where they are already hanging out (virtually). Join groups and/or forums related to your niche online. This will allow you to network with others who may be able to help with your business or bounce ideas off of. It's also a great way of getting feedback on new ideas or products before launching them into the market! Understand which social platforms your customers are using so you know where to make your presence known the most.

Raving customers and fans of your business are invaluable. Referrals from your existing clients are one of the best ways to generate new leads, because it's a win-win-win situation for everyone involved: the past customer shares a business they love, the new customer gets a great product or service recommended by someone they trust, and you get the opportunity to expand your business by taking on new clients. Here are some tips to help you make the most of your existing client base:

If you haven't been asking for referrals yet, the time to start is **yesterday**. Whenever you interact with a current or past client — whether by email, phone call or in person - ask if they know anyone else who could benefit from your services. Make this a habit so that it becomes second nature when talking with clients. Don't be afraid to ask! People love to feel like they are part of a community rather than just another transaction.

Past client testimonials are marketing gold; there's nothing better than someone selling your product (for free) - without you spending any additional time or money. This is exactly what happens when you have a solid understanding of how best to help your customers; they are far more likely to rave about your products/services/company to others. These testimonials (whether written, audio or video) should be easily available to your prospects on your website, social platforms and can even be used in digital ads.

the best products and services facilitate **transformation.**

the best brands **stand for something**.

successful prospecting

RESEARCH. A LOT.

ASK CLARIFYING QUESTIONS

BE CURIOUS WHEN YOU ASK QUESTIONS

IF YOU DON'T UNDERSTAND, MIRROR

REPEAT THE LAST 3-5 WORDS THEY SAID

COREY BERRIER

I am about to share with you a simple but powerful discovery tool I have used to make millions of dollars:

Imagine you walk into a doctors office, and without asking a single question about what your symptoms are or where your pain is... they recommend immediate surgery. Not only would this be ridiculously unprofessional, it shows a total lack of compassion or willingness to care about you as an individual.

If you haven't completed steps 1-3, you're probably not asking the right questions when qualifying a lead. If you place more value on your paycheck than your service, or if you have un(der)qualified prospects, you're leaving money on the table. And, of course, if you underdeliver you are doing a disservice to your existing and potential customers, as well as your own business. On the other hand, when you know yourself, your business and your target customer, you'll be starting the process ten steps ahead.

Before you can implement an unbeatable discovery method, you have to make sure you are prospecting in the right places (which is why that step comes first).

The first step is becoming a student of your customers' current environment because you need to understand their wants, needs and pain points. Then you can position yourself as the ultimate solution to their problem.

> Once you understand your ideal customer's needs and challenges, you can begin asking questions; focus on those that will help you uncover how you can provide them with the most value.

Here are some examples:

- What are their biggest challenges?
- What problems do they struggle with?
- What do they think about their current vendor(s)?
- What products/services would they like to see from us?

use your **purpose** to craft your perfect offer

One of the most important things I've learned as a SME is there are two kinds of work: **doing what matters and everything else**. I've found that a common challenge for entrepreneurs is figuring out what matters most to them. I'm not referring to the obvious things like making money, having an impact, or building a great team; I'm talking about what matters most to you personally. The next step is figuring out how to make it happen — **how to do what matters most** — in your life and in your business.

When do you feel most alive? When do you feel like fully yourself? When and where do you accomplish the most?

These questions can help you find your zone of genius.

(discussed further on the next page)

Once you know your purpose, you can take action towards it in a way that feels authentic and energizing - even if it doesn't fit someone else's idea of success (or yours). Your purpose becomes your fuel; it allows you to use what matters to you to help humanize your sales process. And... guess what?

It's also what resonates most with your target audience.

zone of genius

I want to talk about a phrase that you may or not be familiar with; your **zone of genius**. No, I'm not talking about people who are human calculators - it's actually something that every single person has (whether they know it or not).

So, what is your zone of genius? It's the area where you are best at doing something. It's not necessarily what you enjoy doing, and it's not necessarily what people might expect from you. But, it's where you can make a difference, feel the most fulfilled, and where your gifts are put to best use.

If we're honest with ourselves, we can find our zone of genius by reflecting on our wins and accomplishments, our skills and interests, and simply what makes us happy — even if it's just a good day at work. When we do this exercise, we sometimes realize that our zone of genius isn't exactly what we thought it was.

When we are able to do what matters, we feel alive — we connect with something bigger than ourselves, something that gives our lives meaning. You need to '**discover**' yourself before you can connect with your ideal customers.

know you can **win.**

show your **customers** you're a winner.

use your **purpose** to amplify your **connection** with your audience.

powerful discovery

DO YOU BELIEVE WHAT YOU DO MATTERS? WHY?

WHAT DOES SUCCESS LOOK LIKE FOR YOU?

WHAT IS YOUR ZONE OF GENIUS

HOW CAN YOUR PURPOSE HELP YOU CONNECT WITH YOUR AUDIENCE

four

COREY BERRIER

If you have a perfect offer it will be irresistible to your target audience. If there is a hotdog stand outside of a bar at 2 AM, they're going to sell out of hotdogs. If that hotdog stand set up outside a vegan festival.... well, you get it.

As I mentioned earlier, knowing your customer is vital to connecting with them. That connection makes crafting an offer far more likely to land. You need to pick up on your prospect's cue to figure out what their wants, needs and expectations are. Crafting the 'perfect' offer is an art, and will be unique to each individual making their pitch. It will usually evolve with time as you become more confident in your process and more understanding of your audience.

Instead of struggling to present the value, present an offer that closes itself. Or, to paraphrase a certain movie... **'make them an offer they can't refuse'**. If they are refusing, move on - *STOP CHASING TIRE KICKERS*! Your goal should be to construct an offer that gives you a **HELL YES** (not an OK, maybe later).

Before I tell you how to go about constructing your own perfect offer, let's look at what **NOT** to do.

what does a bad offer look like?

- **CONFUSING**
  No organized process + no explanation = no sale.

- **BORING**
  If you're not excited, your prospects wont be either. You cant help customers imagine what life will look and feel like when they buy.
  Facts tell and stories sell.

- **UNCONVINCING**
  Your leads may think that they (or someone else) knows more than you about the product/service. Alternatively, the excitement, intrigue and/or value is not there (so the sale wont be either).

Every business wants to increase sales, but often forget that a sale always starts with an offer. If you focus only on the result ($), you'll have a harder time getting it. If you've been in business for a while, then you know that it's not as simple as just knocking on doors or cold calling and asking people to buy your product or service. Your message should be clear and your offer irresistible.

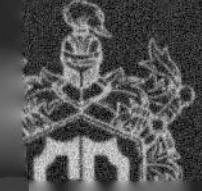

crafting **your** perfect offer

I am going to share with you a **proven** three-step process that will help you craft your offer to close consistently.

In the most simplest of terms, your offer needs to be compelling enough that people will want to pay for it; **you need an offer that closes**. Work through these steps in order to craft an offer that works for you and your business.

process

Every business should have a unique process for fulfilling their orders from lead to happy customer. The first thing you need to do is define **what** makes up your offer, and the best way to **deliver** it. This includes how you word your sales copy/script, how you overcome objections and to handle indecisive buyers. You should also plan out exactly what happens on your customer's journey after the deal is closed.

emotion

Your offer should be tied closely to what makes people want something in the first place: **emotions**. People buy products that make them feel good about themselves, help them to solve a problem, or accomplish something important in their lives. When you tie emotion into your offer it becomes more than just words or a promise; it makes people *feel something*. It creates a **connection**, which is more important now than ever. If your offer resonates on an emotional level more than your competitors', the customer is far more likely to choose you.

value > cost

The last step is figuring out how to offer the most value. You need to clearly showcase that you are providing more value than the amount of money they are spending. This is especially important when presenting fixed price packages (rather than hourly rates). If someone pays $300 for your service package, but you explain that it will save them $1000 in lost time and aggravation, they'll recognize that added value instantly. Even offering free shipping or some kind of "limited time offer" can increase conversions by up to 50%.

Unless you are in some kind of unicorn market with zero competition, there are a lot of others selling what you're selling. **You need to provide a unique value proposition that sets you apart from your competitors.**

the perfect offer
CLARIFY YOUR OFFER
ADD MORE VALUE
ANALYZE COMPETITOR OFFERS
WHAT IS UNIQUE ABOUT YOUR OFFER?

#6 objection crusher

If I told you that you could increase your closing success by 20% just by losing your fear of rejection, would you believe it?

There is actually scientific evidence that people can unconsciously detect whether someone is stressed or scared by smelling a chemical pheromone released in their sweat. If you'd like to learn more about this somewhat gross but definitely interesting study (it involved novice skydivers and armpit sweat), google Dr Lilianne Mujica-Parodi at Stony Brook University. Beyond smell, though, I'm sure you can remember a time when you sensed that someone was nervous or uncomfortable. If your prospect suspects you are - in any way - uncertain about what you are selling, the chance of you closing that deal drops significantly.

The good news is, (**if you have completed the first 3 steps in order**) you have an increased understanding of your customers' needs and wants. This will position you to anticipate and overcome objections quicker and easier than ever before - sometimes before they even think them!

you really **can** crush objections <u>before they exist</u>.

One of the biggest struggles when it comes to making a deal or selling a product/service is the fear that you wont be able to overcome an objection. Ironically, **it is this fear that makes it more likely to happen**.

To avoid this, it's pretty simple; know your sh**!! If someone asked you to talk about how you brush your teeth, you wouldn't have any issues answering their questions, because you do it every day. When you know what you're talking about, it doesn't matter who asks what, or how they ask it. You don't even need to think of the answer; it will be automatic! There's nothing worse than a potential customer asking you something about your business that you don't have an answer to. Know yourself, know your business, and be prepared for each interaction.

BUT... it's not all about you.

being confident to crush objections doesn't mean focusing only on your side of the conversation.

If you're not really listening to what your customer is asking or saying, you're going to have a hard time overcoming their objections. You are also far more likely to come off as aloof or ignorant; the prospect is going to feel like 'just another customer' rather than a person, and will be less likely to do business with you.

OBJECTION CRUSHER CHEAT SHEET

- ✓ ASK THE RIGHT QUESTIONS
- ✓ SHOW THEM YOU ACTUALLY CARE
- ✓ INTUITIVE/ACTIVE LISTENENING
- ✓ MIRROR BODY AND TONE
- ✓ THINK AHEAD

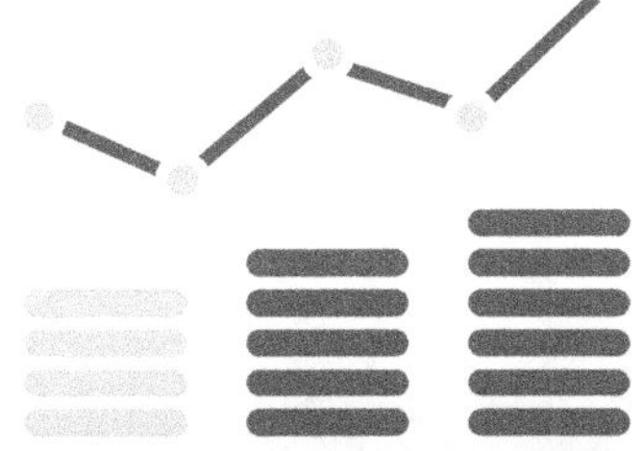

5 communication tips to help you crush objections:

ASK THE RIGHT QUESTIONS

Once again, I'm reminding you to ask (the right) questions! When handling objections, choose open-ended and clarifying questions like "how can I help you?" and "what is it you're looking to get from (xyz)?", rather than simple yes/no questions.

SHOW THEM YOU ACTUALLY CARE

Use phrases like "I see" or "tell me more. These phrases show that you're engaged in what they're saying. This will make them feel valued and respected — two things that are key when dealing with people who may be skeptical or nervous about making a purchase decision - especially when it's from someone they don't know well yet (or at all).

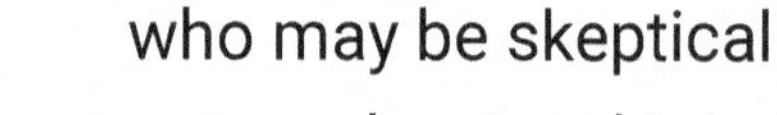

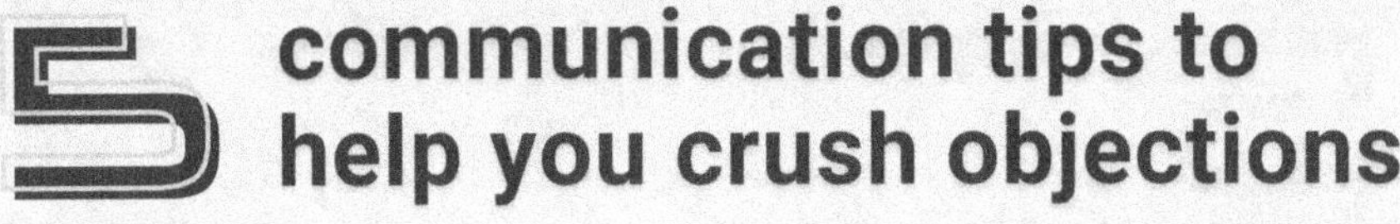

Understand the **root** of the objection; sometimes people just don't understand how something works. Other times they may be hesitant because of budget constraints or other factors outside of your control. That's when empathy comes in handy: acknowledge their concerns without getting defensive about them, and move on from there as quickly as possible. That way, both parties can get back on track (instead of making things more awkward than they already are!)

INTUITIVE/ACTIVE LISTENENING

Listen with intent – not just with your ears, but with your eyes and intuition. Pay attention to the words coming out of their mouth, how they're moving around and how their tone changes when discussing certain topics (i.e., when answering a question about why they want to lower their payments).

MIRROR BODY AND TONE

One of the easiest ways to build rapport and trust with someone is to mirror their body language and tone. As you listen to them, watch how they act. Analyze their body language, energy and mood and try to replicate it. Not only will this improve your connection with them, but it will also help ensure that they feel comfortable around you!

You'll find that by simply paying attention to these subtle cues from others (while making sure not to overdo it), both sides will be able to connect on a deeper level - they will feel understood. These steps, even before a sale, marks the beginning of your customer relationship.

THINK AHEAD

One of the best ways to anticipate and counter objections is by thinking ahead. Think about the objections that would most likely come up, make a list of them and then create a script for how to handle each one. Practice your script with a friend or family member until it becomes second nature for you. Research online in groups and forums to see if you can sniff out any clues about common objections. If you've planned ahead, even if someone raises an objection right when you're about to close... you'll be prepared!

Don't let an objection turn into an argument. People have different tastes and preferences; especially when dealing with luxury items like cars or jewelry that cost tens (or hundreds) thousands dollars apiece!

Remember, these tips are just a framework; it's essential for you to add you own personal touch in order for it to come across as legitimate and authentic.

objection crusher

PRACTICE ACTIVE LISTENING

PRACTICE HOW TO RESPOND

ROLEPLAY WITH A FRIEND OR FAMILY MEMBER

RESEARCH COMMON OBJECTIONS

PLAN AHEAD

When you're closing a deal, it comes down to this simple fact (that you may or may not want to hear): **you have to ask for the money, because if you don't your competition will**. If you wait for your customer to ask for a price quote or for a commitment to buy, you are leaving the door open for someone else to make that call first.

There are a few ways you can close a sale and each one has different strengths and weaknesses. The method you use should depend on what kind of product or service you're selling and the type of client you're dealing with. But why do so many people struggle with this part? Chances are you could be getting in your own way!

Fear - You avoid asking for the money (the sale). You think people will run.

Scarcity - You think there are not enough customers so you try to close every deal (but never ask for referrals).

ABC - You are not Alec Baldwin. Always Be Closing does not work.

Another reason closing can be challenging is because it usually occurs at the end of a long process that includes a number of steps. The length of time each step varies on a case-by-case basis, but the process should look somehing like this:

- Build rapport and **trust** with your prospect
- Identify **needs** and **problems**
- Educate your prospect about your solution
- Demonstrate how your product or service is their ultimate solution
- Ask for the order 

Ask **directly:** When it comes time to close, don't be afraid to ask directly for what you want — don't beat around the bush or dance around the issue. Just get straight to the point.

Rinse and repeat: As you likely already know, "no" doesn't always mean no when it comes to a sale. It could mean they're not quite convinced yet, or need more information.

It really comes down to two main things you need: a **clear understanding** of your goal and a **willingness to risk** getting rejected by asking for what you want. If your offer is priced reasonably and the value proposition is clear (and legitimate), you can leave fear at the door; you can be confident in what you're offering because you constructed it to be that way. If someone flat out objects to your offer, they are likely not the person to chase!

Ultimately, the best way to ask for the money is by doing it at the right time and in the right way. Be confident in your process and prequalify your prospects to give yourself the best shot at a quick and easy close!

It's not about hard-core closing; it's about providing a **valuable solution** for your customer for a reasonable exchange for money.

Operate consistently, so you have predictable sales. That's when you grow your business and become a leader in your industry.

closing the deal

DON'T FEAR YOUR OWN PITCH

MAKE THE VALUE CLEAR

SHOW YOU UNDERSTAND THEIR HESITATIONS:

"TELL ME MORE?"

"SEEMS LIKE..."

"SOUNDS LIKE..."

COREY BERRIER

I'll share a story with you about a $54,000 project that I almost didn't get because I didn't follow up. Why? Because I told myself she didn't want to do business with me. Well, that reality existed in my mind only; she actually just wanted one more thing added to the contract before she signed it.

If I believed my self-sabotaging story instead of following up (and sticking to my proven process), I would have missed out on $54,000. Following up is **key**.

Follow up with your leads quickly after finding them (and regularly after!). You want them to feel like you care about them and want their business. This can be done by email or text, sending a calendar link to book a call, and actually getting on the call! Effective follow up allows you to build a relationship with your prospect and helps you understand their needs, wants and desires even more.

You need to have a separate follow up process that begins at the point of purchase, for each and every sale you make.

Luckily, there are a few strategies you can implement that crossover for both following up with a lead and a paying customer.

humanize the process

I hope it goes without saying, but **be polite**. You'd be amazed how much basic manners can go a long way in creating a positive relationship with someone—especially when they're the one who has something that could benefit your business. If you're in an industry that has some not-so-great stereotypes and preconceived notions; make sure it's clear from your first interaction (and every subsequent one) that you care about your customers and want to help them however you can.

Be **personal**. The best way to do this is by using their name. If you're not sure what their name is, ask! They'll appreciate it and you'll feel more connected with them as a result.

Try to use **names** frequently in your communication, both theirs and yours! It shows them that you are an actual human being and not just an automated email bot. It shows the lead that you see them as a human not just a potential sale. It's also easier for us to remember things when we know how they relate to ourselves (like "that person who always remembers my name").

consistent cadence

The best way to ensure a lead converts to a customer is consistent follow up. After you have sent your first email, you should schedule weekly or bi-weekly emails in which you provide value and ask if they need any assistance. The right cadence will depend on your product or service as well as your audience. Some businesses may need to follow up every couple of months, other businesses send out weekly updates, or you may find that a few times a week is the best number. So how can you determine what timeframe is too infrequent vs spammy? There are several factors that must be considered:

- Does your audience work during specific hours? When are they most active on social platforms? Try to schedule your communications during a time they are likely to see and/or respond
- What time zone does your audience live in? If most of them are based overseas (for example, Europe), then afternoon US time would probably work better than evening US time - many employees will still be at work but not yet going home for dinner at 6pm Eastern Standard Time (EST).
- For leads, you likely want to shorten the time between communications. This is how you nurture a lead into a paying customer. But, **no one wants to be spammed**. Never communicate with a lead more than 1x/day (the exception would be a multi-day program that would involve more frequent check-ins, etc.)

don't **spam**

Being "spammy" goes beyond overwhelming an inbox; don't use **spammy language**. This is easy to do when you're excited and want to share your message, but it's important that you don't send out an email or tweet that sounds like a scam or sales pitch from a telemarketer. Your followers are smart people who can tell if something is too good to be true, so don't waste their time by trying to sell them on something too quickly.

Avoid sending **spammy content**. If someone is following you for updates about your business or blog posts about your industry, then sending them updates all day long will get boring quickly, and they'll likely unfollow you in favor of someone who doesn't send as much information. Sometimes the best follow up content provides almost only value with no selling, or with maybe just a "ps. here is a link to something".

Lastly, don't spam anyone with multiple messages at once; this includes tweets and emails as well as DMs (but DMs are an excellent way to connect with your potential and current customers)! Never send more than one message per channel at any given time - unless there's truly something urgent going on, like breaking news or a last-minute offer. You don't want people thinking there's always something urgent going on; they may unfollow because they feel like they're constantly being sold something instead of getting real value from what they were initially drawn to.

how can I **help**?

Most of all, do not forget to ask if they need anything else. It doesn't need to (and shouldn't) be pushy, but don't forget to ask if there is anything more you can help them with. Ask this question at the end of the conversation, when you're wrapping up and preparing to say goodbye.

If they say no, thank them again for their time and wish them well on their journey with your product!

If they say yes... then it's time to offer an alternative solution that might better fit their needs. Don't suggest things that are completely unrelated or outside of your wheelhouse - but do always offer them something else so that you can build a long-term relationship with this customer instead of just selling him or her once and forgetting about you!

every single customer
wants to know you care.

show them.

effective
follow-up

DON'T BE A SPAMMER

DON'T BE A GHOST

CONSISTENCY NOT
OVERWHELM

STAY TOP OF MIND

FOLLOW UP - SALE OR NOT

HUMANIZE THE PROCESS

Scaling your business is important, but if you attempt to do it preemptively or in the wrong way, it's going to have the opposite affect you want. When people try to scale their business before it's time, they scale mediocrity, and nobody wants to scale mediocrity. I see that happen more times than you'd believe, and here are a few other struggles associated with scaling a business (even when it's ready!):

hero complex

Firefighting constant problems is not heroic; it is bad management. The hero complex is when you feel like you need to be an expert at everything. You constantly fix problems yourself when there are other people who could be doing the work better (and maybe faster) than you. This leads to poor delegation which almost always causes burnout and micromanagement issues. If you find yourself constantly having to fix things, it might be time to analyze how your company operates. Consider outsourcing any tasks that you do not enjoy or are not best equipped to handle. You may feel that if you delegate you are giving up. **It's the opposite**, really. Smart delegation is essential to scale your business, otherwise you'll burn yourself out before you see the results you want. The goal is to create a sales system that generates consistent, reliable revenue - without losing your money or sanity.

ego

You are bottlenecking yourself. If you're feeling like nobody else can do what you do, this might be your problem. This kind of thinking will not help you grow your business, and you will never find the people who are actually right for that job. If this is an issue for you, you are also far less likely to collaborate with others in your industry (big mistake!).

disorganized

This one's pretty simple; a disorganized business will never reach it's full potential.

Once you've found a system that works and has been proven to be profitable, THEN you can start to scale the business. Start bringing on more people and use tools to help them work more efficiently. Use outsourcing where appropriate to get tasks done more effectively by others. Automate processes as much as possible so you can focus on what matters most: closing deals and growing your sales team! And of course, **collaboration** is a great way to scale your business and reach a new audience! Don't be afraid to reach out to others in your industry - it will benefit both parties!

Make short and long term goals, and reevaluate them consistently. If you aren't hitting targets, quickly determine why that is. When you find a system that works, see how you can implement it in other aspects of your business.

so...
do you want to grow a
mess or scale success?

scale your business

DON'T SCALE MEDIOCRITY

OUTSOURCE ANYTHING THAT MAKES SENSE

ANALYZE YOUR COMPETITION AND INDUSTRY REGULARLY

COLLABORATE WITH OTHERS

DEVELOP A 'SET AND FORGET SYSTEM'

When I was eight years old I was diagnosed with ADHD. Up until nine months ago, I had no idea what that really meant for me. I was taking medicine yes, but I didn't really know I had executive function disorders (or anything about what they really are).

I didn't know that it was normal for me to forget things. I didn't know it was normal for me to leave my phone in the freezer and look for it for 20 minutes. I didn't know it was normal for me to not follow through on things I don't really care. One of the most difficult (but definitely cathartic) thing for me to acknowledge was that sometimes I don't follow through even on things I really do care about. This lack of awareness lead to a ton of self-critical and negative energy towards myself... not healthy!

Now, I am on a mission to let people know about attention deficit hyperactivity disorder, because I lived with it for 36 years basically untreated. I have since interviewed over 50 ADHD professionals; what I found is MOST entrepreneur's have ADHD and most sales people have ADHD. I found this fascinating and wanted to find any resources that would offer some insight - what is the connection with an ADHD mind and a career in sales and/or being an entrepreneur? So, what did I find?

absolutely nothing.

This is the first book ever written that really gets into ADHD and how it relates to sales and entrepreneurs. This BLEW MY MIND, especially since individuals with ADHD seem to excel in the sales industry far more than other professions. The lack of resources was a huge factor for why I felt I had to include it in this book.

You may be wondering why the title of this section is "**free thinkers**" rather than specifically naming "ADHD". The reason is simple; the symptoms and challenges that come with ADHD are not exclusive to those with an actual diagnosis. There is a large crossover between what I and others "ADHDers" struggle with, and those who may just think a bit differently. If you are neurodivergent in any way, or have ever been described as "spirited", "energetic", (or maybe in a negative manner like) "unhinged" or a "loose cannon", this section is very likely to benefit you!

ADD or ADHD?

In 1994, the medical community decided all forms of Attention - Deficit Disorder would now be classified as "Attention-Deficit/Hyperactivity Disorder; **ADHD**. Those diagnosed today who do not suffer with hyperactivity receive the same ADHD diagnosis as someone who does. For the purpose of distinguishing between the two in this section I will use both acronyms. Because I have been medically diagnosed, I will be writing specifically about using your ADHD to achieve more success in your business, but again - **if you do not have a diagnosis you will still benefit from the tips and tools provided**.

more than "**just hyper**"

Just like ADD, ADHD is a type of attention disorder, and it is much more than just that hyper kid in school (as it is often portrayed in the media). It is a spectrum, and one that involves both obstacles and abilities. No two people present the exact same challenges and gifts. It also presents quite differently in males vs. females.

Some people with ADHD have severe difficulty paying attention because they simply can't stay focused. Many feel restless as a result, and bounce around from activity to activity (or task to task). Other people with ADHD may just feel like they're scatterbrained because their mind wanders - they get distracted easily by noise, lights or other stimuli, and have trouble concentrating on tasks that require sustained focus. In these cases, they need external help (which comes n many forms, like to-do lists, journaling, therapy) in order to organize their thoughts and actions better. Then they can complete projects more effectively without being overwhelmed by distractions.

Everyone is different; there isn't just one way for those with ADD/ADHD brains work best - but I'm going to offer a few recommendations. Find what works best for YOU and then stick to it. I wouldn't be here today if I hadn't done just that.

is it really a **gift**?

You may have heard that "it's a gift, not a disorder". That is absolutely true for some people, but not all. As with any gift, it only helps you if you use it right!

There are, in fact, many benefits to having ADHD. For starters, people with ADHD have a very high level of creative thinking. They think outside the box and see things in new ways, which is an excellent tool to have in business. It can be hard for someone without ADHD to understand this different way of thinking, but I like to say it feels like your brain works at lightning speed (whether you want it to or not)! This enables people with ADHD to solve problems before others may even know they exist. It also means you have a higher likelihood of detecting and crushing objections before your lead can get it out of their mouth.

Another great benefit of having ADHD is that we are able to focus on multiple tasks at once - even if they're completely unrelated! People without ADHD often find this overwhelming or impossible; their brains cannot function fast or vast enough for more than one thing at once (at least not without being seriously stressed out). ADHDers are usually motivated by accomplishments and milestones. It is extremely helpful to write out the goals you want to have and a desired timeline. You can use your energy and drive to motivate yourself towards achieving these goals faster - both when working alone and within teams.

hyper**focus**

Hyperfocus is a lesser known but very common symptom associate with ADHD. The term describes being intensely and single-mindedly concentrated on one thing. It can be incredibly useful in certain situations, but it can also have its drawbacks.

We'll start with the bad news. To start, here's a VERY common misconception held by those who first learn about this term: *hyperfocus... like, I can just focus really good and get a lot of stuff done, that's a good thing right?*

Unfortunately, it's not that simple. Hyperfocus can be so intense that you **literally cannot focus on anything else**. This means if you're not careful, you might forget to eat lunch, important events or you may even forget go home at the end of the day. In extreme cases, it can lead to bladder infections because yes - you may be so focused on what you're doing you forget to go to the bathroom. Analyze how intense your focus is when you're working, and be sure to prioritize your health and wellbeing, <u>ALWAYS</u>. This is especially true for women with ADHD; they often put themselves at the bottom of their priority list. *Fun fact: the designer of this book, a fellow ADHDer, requested I emphasize this point. For her, this was the most difficult hurdle to overcome when starting her business.* **You really can't pour from an empty cup**. Cheesy phrase? Sure, but true nonetheless. Growing your business can be a top priority, but you need to be there to enjoy the ride! Please keep this in mind, throughout every step of the process.

Okay, onto the GOOD NEWS!! Being able to hyperfocus **absolutely has its advantages**. When you're hyperfocused on a project or task, you get really into what you're doing. Your brain is working at maximum capacity. You see potential obstacles, you understand every single piece of the puzzle, and can really get creative with building solutions and strategies.

So what does this mean for your business? If you're going into an interview or presentation that requires a lot of mental energy, then yes: hyperfocus could be an asset for you! If instead you need to multitask during these types of situations (which often happens), then maybe not so much. Start analyzing the various scenarios involved with your business, and decide where and when you should put your hyperfocus to work. It's important to remember that (ADHD or not) everyone has different strengths and weaknesses; those strengths will vary depending on what type of environment they're working in.

The more aware you are of your external environment and your internal response, the better you'll be able to navigate each scenario in a way that works best for you.

imagine more

An overactive imagination is very common among ADHDers and free thinkers. When you are a kid and meant to sit still all day long in school, you're often discourage to 'day dream' and reminded over and over to stay focused.

I am here to say to you: let your imagination run wild! If you're having trouble with a problem, ask yourself the question, "what if I did this?" or "what if we did that?" Play out different scenarios and outcomes in your mind, pick the one you like best and start thinking about how to make it happen.

Be creative in your thinking, but don't forget to welcome ideas from others. If you're an individual contributor and are trying to solve a problem that can't be solved by one person alone, work with others on the team who have different perspectives than yours and are willing to brainstorm together as equals. Brainstorm with your team members, friends, family and even your customers/followers. You never know what someone could say that could spark the perfect idea in your mind.

A note of caution: If you have this kind of hyperactive imagination, be sure to keep it in check; it doesn't do any good to imagine (and ultimately hyperfocus) on all of the potential horrible things that could happen! Try to organize and manage that wild imagination as much as you can, so you can harness it to create incredible things, not torture you!

choose the **right industry**

I believe that ADHD is a career asset when it comes to sales for a few reasons: Sales involves persuading others, which is something that people with ADHD are innately good at. They can sell just about anything because they think outside of the box.

Certain industries value creativity more than others, and you may find that you thrive more going down one of those paths. If you are a risk taker than choose an industry that encourage (or at least allow) people to try new things! Some examples of such industries include advertising, marketing and public relations; art; film; music; fashion design; sports coaching and management; programming; finance.

But remember, free thinkers have an uncanny ability to think outside the box; you can make just about anything work if you try hard/long enough. Ultimately, no matter which path you choose to take, whether starting something new or building on an existing foundation, I want you to read these words and remember them:

If you put in the work you are destined for success. You have the drive, you have the creativity, you have the courage. You just have to trust yourself to take that leap and go all in... on anything and everything you want!

just the beginning...

In the past 25 years I have seen SO many businesses struggling to make sales and/or failing to get their message to resonate with their customers. I quickly realized I could provide even more solutions to businesses looking for a partner to help them solve problems, no matter how large or small.

All the tips, tools and strategies provided in this guide will set you up for better organization, more success and help you position your business to be ready to scale exponentially. BUT, remember to always focus **WHY** you're in this business; otherwise none of that will matter.

If you want a coach in your corner helping you set and annihilate your sales goals, build effective strategies and processes while still having time and a life to do the things that are most important to you, click the button below.

I can't wait to help you
and your business reach
maximum potential.

– COREY BERRIER

I'M READY

SELL MORE $H!T

COREY BERRIER

www.ingramcontent.com/pod-product-compliance
Lightning Source LLC
Chambersburg PA
CBHW061433050726
47593CB00006B/2329